KNOWLEDGE ENCYCLOPEDIA

ANCIENT & MEDIEVAL ARCHITECTURE

© Wonder House Books 2021

All rights reserved. No part of this book may be reproduced or transmitted in any form by any means, electronic or mechanical, including photocopying and recording, or by any information storage and retrieval system except as may be expressly permitted in writing by the publisher.

(An imprint of Prakash Books)

contact@wonderhousebooks.com

Disclaimer: The information contained in this encyclopedia has been collated with inputs from subject experts. All information contained herein is true to the best of the Publisher's knowledge.

ISBN : 9789390391486

Table of Contents

Ageless Architecture	3
Folk Architecture	4–5
The First Cities	6–7
The Wonders of Ancient Egypt	8–9
Classical Greece	10–11
Classical Rome	12–13
Byzantine Splendour	14–15
Chinese Architecture	16–17
Islamic Architecture	18–19
Architecture of the Indian Subcontinent	20–21
Heritage of Southeast Asia	22–23
Dynamic Japan	24
Japanese Gardens	25
Pre-Columbian Americas	26–27
Romanesque Architecture	28–29
Gothic Architecture	30–31
Word Check	32

AGELESS **ARCHITECTURE**

The American master builder Louis Kahn called architecture the 'thoughtful making of space'. Our earliest buildings were so well made that we can still see and explore their amazing remains. Some are so strangely constructed that modern architects cannot figure out how they were made.

Inspiration for early architecture came from wars, religious beliefs and sacred practices. Inspired by their faith in Christ, medieval Europeans built soaring cathedrals. In the east, a closeness with nature led to buildings set in large, entrancing gardens. Ancient Egyptians stored the remains of kings along with their treasures in towering pyramids. Ancient Romans built columns and arches celebrating the victories of the Roman Empire. All across the globe, ancient and medieval architecture reflects the remarkable stories of human endeavour.

▼ *Built during the Ming Dynasty, the Forbidden City is the vast, amazing palace complex of Imperial China*

Folk Architecture

In many parts of the world, people still build houses using ancient and traditional designs. For instance, certain barn styles in America were first seen in Europe in the 1st millennium BCE! This kind of folk architecture used local materials. It meets only the most basic needs of human beings. It is generally built by local workers, not by formally trained architects. The designs are cheap, dependable and have thus remained unchanged through the centuries.

◀ Poplar Cottage in Sussex, England belonged to a 15th-century shoemaker. Only the hall in this house was heated. The fire burned in a 'smoke bay' (not a chimney). The ground floor had the 'shop', while the two rooms upstairs were bedrooms

▲ In Bronze Age Sardinia, people built round fortresses called nuraghi. These were often surrounded by a hive of round stone houses. The whole structure was walled off together as a single architectural unit

◀ The pastoral Toda people of India live in small groups along green slopes. Their thatched houses are built on a wooden framework in the shape of a half barrel

 Climate

Among the most important factors affecting folk architecture is the local climate. Buildings in cold regions are generally thick, low and covered in insulation. Windows are either small or non-existent. Doors are always tightly sealed to keep the indoors warm. Buildings in hot, dry places focus on cross-ventilation and cooling fixtures, such as screens, gardens and water features. Areas that face heavy monsoons, tides or flooding have homes that are raised off the ground.

▼ The Musgum people build amazing huts with baked clay in the flood plains between northern Cameroon and Chad, Africa

ANCIENT & MEDIEVAL ARCHITECTURE

Windcatchers

Windcatchers are traditional **ventilation** towers of the arid Middle East. The towers often have screens that can be sprayed with water. The water evaporates and cools the air that passes down the tower to the rooms below.

Mashrabiya

Projecting windows (oriels) are excellent ventilators. They are usually found in an upper storey. In the Islamic world, these are not covered by panes. Rather, to let in fresh air and soft light, they have beautiful lattices and grills. Such oriels are called mashrabiya.

In Real Life

The Inuits of Canada and Greenland build temporary winter villages. Their dome-shaped dwellings made of snow-bricks are called igloos. In summer, the Inuit live in sealskin tents.

▲ An Inuit village of igloos

◀ Two rows of exquisite mashrabiya at the caravanserai of Bazaara, in a medieval part of Cairo, Egypt. Mashrabiya are plentiful across the cities of the Middle East and North Africa. During colonial times, they were introduced to France as moucharabieh (moucharaby in English)

Building Materials

Folk architecture draws on local resources. It shows great variety and creativity in the use of common materials like granite, sandstone and timber. **Adobe** is one such popular material. It is a heavy, earthy mixture used to make sun-dried bricks. It can be made using clay, sand, silt and even straw. Another amazing material is cob. This is made of wet earth and organic matter such as hay. The mixture is rolled into loaf-sized blocks called cobs.

Waterproof structures use thatch and tiles. Thatch is crafted by braiding or packing together dry vegetation. This could be straw, reeds, rushes, heather or palm fronds. Traditional tiles are made from fired clay. They are excellent for a wide range of climates and purposes. Nomadic people need mobile homes. These are generally made from skins and pelts stitched together into tents.

▲ A cob building in Morocco; this clay-like material is easily moulded to give curving structures, and inbuilt features like shelves and hooks. Windows could be cut anywhere into the wall

The First Cities

The oldest extant ruins of a city date back to the 5th millennium BCE. Located in modern Iran, this city is called Eridu. It was home to the Ubaid civilisation. Eridu is known for its numerous temples, made of technologically advanced (for its era) mud-brick architecture. Most early cities were built during the Bronze Age, around the time writing was invented. City-building began in earnest in Mesopotamia, the Cradle of Civilisation. Mesopotamian architecture consists of the buildings of Sumer, Akkadia, Assyria and Babylonia. Sumerian cities are most likely the oldest, and date from c. 3100 BCE.

▲ An artist's imagination of the Port of Eridu

▲ 19th-century dig to find the ancient buried Babylonian city of Nippur

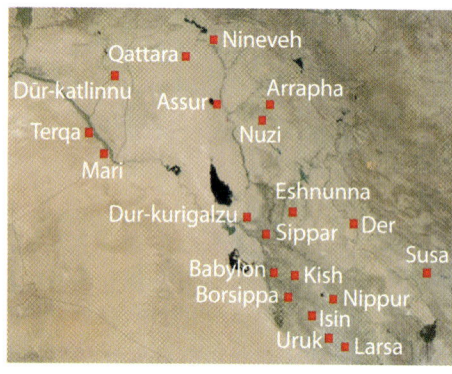
▲ Prominent cities of Lower Mesopotamia in the 2nd millennium BCE

In Real Life

The Biblical Tower of Babel is often thought to be the legendary seven-tiered ziggurat of the great temple of Marduk, in Babylon.

▲ A fantastical 16th-century painting of the Hanging Gardens of Babylon, with the Tower of Babel in the background

Ziggurat

Mesopotamian architecture is famous for ziggurats which are rectangular stepped towers with temples at the top. Architects used mud bricks to build the ziggurat core. They covered the exterior with baked bricks. Unlike Egyptian pyramids, there are no chambers within a ziggurat. Uniquely, trees and shrubs were grown on the massive slopes and terraces of these buildings. This gave rise to the famed Hanging Gardens of Babylon, one of the seven wonders of the ancient world.

The Ziggurat of Ur

Experts know of about 25 ziggurats in the world. They are spread evenly across Sumer, Babylon and Assyria. The best preserved is the ziggurat of Ur. It was completed by the Sumerian King Urnammu and his son Shulgi in around the 21st century BCE. It is a gigantic step pyramid that measures 64 m in length, 46 m in width, and was perhaps over 30 m in height.

▼ Brick ziggurat in Iran

ANCIENT & MEDIEVAL ARCHITECTURE

Indus Valley Civilisation

Around 3000 BCE, the people who lived near the Indus River (modern-day India and Pakistan) began to build cities. Within a millennium, they had some of the most well-planned and hygienic cities, even by today's standards!

The Indus Valley Civilisation first started off as a farming community or settlement. Slowly, they showed signs of urbanisation, i.e. lots of people started living together in a developed town or city. The civilisation comprised of several towns and cities like Mohenjo-Daro and Harappa. They were based along the banks of the Indus River. The quality of life in the Indus Valley was supposedly better than ancient Europe, Babylon and Egypt.

◀ *Ruins of the symmetrically built homes and streets of urban Mohenjo-Daro*

Mohenjo-Daro

One of the largest cities of the Indus Valley was Mohenjo-Daro (Mound of the Dead). On its west was a dominating citadel made of strong mud and bricks, further strengthened by baked bricks. The buildings here included a large tank, a large residence, a massive granary and two assembly halls. The lower town contained regularly laid-out streets that led to houses with courtyards. Amazingly, the houses had indoor bathrooms and drains. Brick stairways suggest they may have had upper stories or flat roofs.

▲ *The Great Bath at Mohenjo-Daro shows the Indus Valley people's love of keeping clean*

💡 Isn't It Amazing!

Though they lived far apart, the Indus Valley people and Mesopotamians had commercial, religious and artistic connections. Some experts think that the Indus Valley people built drains and baths to avoid the squalid, smelly nature of Mesopotamian cities!

▲ *Naksh-e-Rustom is a spectacular necropolis (a burial city for the dead) built into the rock face. It contains the beautifully engraved tombs of seven Persian kings, including the great Darius and Xerxes*

The Wonders of Ancient Egypt

The buildings of ancient Egyptians were so amazing, even their ruins are awe-inspiring. They are characterised by massive works of stone, such as formidable walls, gigantic pyramids and soaring columns. Most surfaces are decorated with **hieroglyphs** and engraved or painted scenes from the lives of ancient Egyptians. This imagery is interspersed with enormous statues of **pharaohs** and mythological gods and beasts.

▲ Statue of Ramesses II at the Temple of Luxor, Karnak

▲ Painted and carved hieroglyphs at the Dendera Temple, Egypt

▲ Hidden behind the formidable sloping walls of this gateway is the magnificent Temple of Horus

Great Temple of Amun-Re

The mesmerising Great Temple of Amun has a dramatic hall of 134 gigantic columns in 16 rows. Each column bears exquisite, detailed carvings along its entire length. In architecture, such a hall, where the roof rests on pillars, is called hypostyle. It means 'under pillars'. The design allowed Egyptian architects to build grand public spaces. The temple itself, with its main portion, was designed and built on an east-west axis in line with a dock. This dock has long since dried though it was reportedly around 100 metre from the Nile river.

◀ Statue of Hatshepsut, the queen who dressed as a man and ruled Egypt in the 15th century BCE

▲ Another set of massive statues of Ramesses II sit regally at the entrance to the Temple of Luxor, Karnak

 Incredible Individuals

High Priest Imhotep was chief minister to King Djoser of Egypt about 5,000 years ago. He designed and built the first pyramid called the Step Pyramid at Sakkara. Imhotep was part of the School of Mysteries of 'The Eye of Horus' that guarded Egypt's knowledge.

▶ Djoser's step pyramid at Sakkara

The Temples of Abu Simbel

Abu Simbel is the complex of two temples built by Ramesses II (ruled 1279–13 BCE). Four gigantic statues of him grace the entrance to the main temple. The temple itself was built to honour the sun gods Amun-Re and Re-Horakhte. It consists of three halls extending for 56 metre into a cliff. These contain statues of the king as Osiris, the god of the afterlife, and paintings of battles. Two days of every year, the first rays of the sun glide through the entire length of the temple and light up the innermost shrine. In the 6th century BCE, Greek adventurers graffitied the sculptures at the temple entrance. This was a gift to experts unearthing the history of the alphabet, especially in relation to Egyptian hieroglyphics.

▶ *The 20-m-high figures of Ramesses at the entrance to Abu Simbel; around the feet are figures of his mother Muttuy, his queen Nefretari, and his children*

The Temple of Hatshepsut

Built by architect Senenmut in the bay, the temple is named after a powerful female pharaoh. The temple was built in c.1473 BCE on three levels, with rows of colonnades and courts. The path to the temple came up the valley through an avenue guarded by sphinxes. The front court was made into a garden of lush trees and vines. Images on the temple walls show stories and scenes from ancient Egypt, such as the marriage of Queen Ahmes to the god Amun-Re and the birth of their child Hatshepsut.

▲ *Deir el-Bahari at Hatshepsut's temple in Egypt*

In Real Life

In the late 1960s, Egypt built the Aswan High Dam on the River Nile. This flooded the land nearby. To prevent ancient Egyptian temples from being submerged, many of them—including Abu Simbel—were moved to other places. In fact, the 2nd-century BCE Debod Temple was shifted entirely out of the country. It now sits on a hill in Spain!

The Pyramids of Giza

The three iconic pyramids of Egypt were constructed during the Fourth Dynasty (c. 2575–2465 BCE). They were named Khufu, Khafre and Menkaure, after the kings who built them. They are made of limestone blocks. They have inner passages and burial chambers for royalty. The pyramid of Khufu is also called the Great Pyramid. It is the oldest of the group, and the largest pyramid ever built. The pyramids were originally covered in white limestone. But over the years, this was hauled away by people to build their own homes. The pyramids no longer shine in the desert sun, as they did once.

▶ *Smaller pyramids around the three giants of Giza are burial monuments for other members of the Egyptian royal family*

Classical Greece

Greek monuments from 1500–350 BCE are known as Classical architecture. The most famous Classical buildings came after 460 BCE. They are part of the golden age of architecture. Among them are gems such as the Parthenon, the Temple of Artemis, and the Theatre of Epidaurus. Classical architecture has elements such as friezes, columns, pediments and caryatids.

▲ A pediment is a narrow triangle just below the roof. Often, it is a platform for decorations called friezes. Here, you see one corner of the pediment of the Parthenon temple. It has a sculpted frieze of a fallen horse and warrior

▲ Caryatids are stone columns in the form of robed maidens. The most famous caryatids are found on the porch of the Erechtheion in the Acropolis

The Acropolis

Greek city centres were built on high ground, to make it difficult for enemies to attack. This centre was called the acropolis. It held all the chief government and religious buildings. The acropolis at Athens was built during the latter part of the 5th century BCE. Dedicated to Athena, the goddess of wisdom and war, it is located on a craggy, walled hill.

▲ The modern-day ruins of Athens' acropolis

▲ The iconic Greek Parthenon at Athens is the goddess Athena's chief shrine

In Real Life

Take a look at the capital (the top) of a Greek column. If it is without any decoration, it is a Doric pillar. If it has a pair of horizontal scrolls, it is an Ionic pillar. If there are beautifully furled sets of leaves, it is a Corinthian column.

Doric Ionic Corinthian

▲ Types of capitals

ANCIENT & MEDIEVAL ARCHITECTURE

The Temple of Artemis

One of the seven wonders of the ancient world, the Temple of Artemis at Ephesus was originally built by King Croesus of Lydia, in 550 BCE. In 356 BCE, it was burned down by a man called Herostratus for the sole purpose of committing a crime. The temple was rebuilt using the original designs. Alexander the Great offered to pay for this work, but the citizens refused him and used their own jewellery to fund the building. It was finally destroyed by invading Goths in 262 CE. The temple was famous for its gargantuan size (about 110 metre by 55 metre) and for many magnificent artworks.

The Temple of Artemis became quite popular in the Renaissance of Europe. There was a coloured engraving prepared by Martin Heemskerck that imagined the temple during the 16th century. In the present day, only a single column remains of the temple, along with other fragments near the site.

▲ Ruins of the Temple of Artemis in Turkey

◀ The Ephesus Artemis was a unique avatar of the goddess, made of gold, ebony, silver and black stone. A 1st-century Roman copy shows her with a high headdress, a multitude of breasts and dressed in a garment with bee motifs

Theatre of Epidaurus

The merchant city of Epidaurus once honoured Asclepius, the god of healing, with a magnificent temple complex. It held temples of Asclepius and Artemis, a stadium, gymnasiums, baths, a hospital and an **abaton**. Its open-air theatre remains an amazing feat of engineering. This is one of the first all-stone Greek theatres ever built. The semi-circular structure is 118 metre in diameter and has 55 rows that can seat up to 13,000 people.

▲ The theatre of Epidaurus is designed in three parts: the auditorium (seating area), the orchestra (the 'dancing floor' or stage) and the skene (a building behind the stage)

⭐ Incredible Individuals

The labyrinthine palace at Knossos with its paintings of bulls probably gave rise to the myths of the Minotaur—the half-man, half-bull son of Pasiphae, wife of King Minos. The Greek hero Theseus was loved by King Minos's daughter. She gave him a spool of thread to mark his way around the Labyrinth. Theseus killed the beast and freed the Athenians, before leaving the island with the King's daughter. King Theseus was the mythical founder of Athens and was compared to the likes of Heracles and Perseus. Athenians held Theseus in great regard, considering him to be a believer of reform. He was also credited with the unification of Athens and Attica.

The Palace of King Minos

Knossos was the centre of an artistic Bronze Age civilisation. The palace here was once a maze-like complex with numerous pillars and stairways. The walls were painted with vibrant frescoes of dancers, dolphins and bulls. The entire area was serviced by carefully built drainage and road networks. Inside the palace, the **gypsum** throne of the kings of Knossos can still be seen.

▶ Painting of a bull at the ruins of the palace at Knossos, Greece

Classical Rome

In the 1st century CE, Rome defeated and took charge of Greece. At the time, it also took Greek culture to heart. With its advanced technologies, Rome was able to take Classical architecture to its peak. The Roman Empire drew architects, masons, craftsmen and ideas from several other civilisations. The result was an explosion of wondrous constructions that reflected wealth and power.

Arches

The development of arches—a feature that can bear great weights—allowed Rome to build massive and multi-level structures. Arches were used in aqueducts, public buildings and even in monuments celebrating great battles.

▲ *The Arch of Constantine (312 CE) was built in memory of a victorious battle. However, most of its sculptures are not original but were taken from older Roman buildings. These included panels, roundels and figures of captives from the time of emperors Domitian, Trajan and Hadrian*

▶ *The Colosseum is a giant public amphitheatre with enormous rows of arches at every level. It could host thousands of Roman spectators, who came to witness fights between gladiators and wild animals*

The Pantheon

An iconic Roman temple, the Pantheon was built and rebuilt by several Roman emperors from 27 BCE onwards. It is a circular monument of concrete. It has a giant dome. The front entrance lies behind tall Corinthian columns. The gates are formed by huge double doors, 27 metre high and made of bronze—the first of their kind. Inside, the Pantheon is lined with coloured marble, granite and semi-precious purple **porphyry**.

▲ *The Pantheon's entrance shows dignified lettering above the columns—an element of proud Roman architecture*

ANCIENT & MEDIEVAL ARCHITECTURE

 ## Urban Rome

Most Roman towns began as well-planned settlements. There would be two main roads, heading north-south and east-west. Public buildings at the centre included markets, the town forum, public baths, arenas, military **barracks** and temples. Many towns also had aqueducts and primitive sewer systems. However, as the empire grew, and towns became cities, town planning was replaced by dirty, noisy urban sprawls and traffic-choked roads.

 ## Thermae

Roman public baths (thermae) had different types of bathing and storage chambers. There was the *apodyterium* (the locker room), the *tepidarium* (a warm room), *caldarium* (a hot room) and *frigidarium* (a cold room).

Isn't It Amazing!

Why is the tomb at Petra called a treasury? As per stories, the Pharaoh, while pursuing Moses, left the great treasures of his army here. The entrance is marred by hundreds of gunshots, made by people who were hunting for the legendary hoard. The true treasure may perhaps be the knowledge from the ancient scrolls that were found at Petra.

▲ Leptis Magna in Libya has well-preserved thermae from the reign of Emperor Hadrian (c. 117–138 CE)

 ## A Rock-cut Treasury

The Treasury (Al-Khazaneh) of the mysterious city of Petra (in Jordan) is actually a spectacular tomb cut into a rock face. Originally a **Nabatean** structure, it was remodelled to Roman tastes after its conquest in 106 CE. They notably added the spectacular Corinthian columns and pediments. The wonderful sunset colour of this rock gives Petra its other name, the rose-red city.

▶ The amazing Library of Celsus was the third richest library of its time. Its grand facade shows decorated, rounded pediments—a step up from the Greek triangular structures

 ## Trajan's Column

This 38-metre-high marble column was erected during 106–113 CE by Emperor Trajan. It is a record of fierce wars that took place between Rome and Germanic tribes. The writing and about 2,000 carvings spiral up the entire length of the column. The **pedestal** contains a chamber that was Trajan's tomb.

▶ Trajan's Column

Byzantine Splendour

At the age of 52, the Roman emperor Constantine I moved away from Rome. He built a new capital in the east and called it Byzantium. After his death, it became famous as Constantinople (now Istanbul). Constantine was also the first Roman emperor to convert to Christianity. His powerful support allowed Christians to make buildings—both secular and religious—that were inspired by their faith. These amazing early Christian works are recognised as Byzantine architecture.

▲ Byzantine architects combined eastern and western designs. Many buildings, such as the spectacular St Mark's Basilica, Venice, had eastern-style domes

The Hagia Sofia

The landmark of Constantinople is the Hagia Sophia (Church of Divine Wisdom). It was built around c. 532–537 CE by Byzantine emperor Justinian I. For almost a thousand years, it was Christendom's largest cathedral. After a couple of earthquakes partly destroyed it, Tradt, the chief architect of the Bagratuni Dynasty in Armenia rebuilt the cathedral in its current form.

▼ The Hagia Sophia Basilica is arranged lengthwise with a central building. The huge saucer-like 32-m dome (second-largest in the world, after the Pantheon's) is supported by twin semi-domes

▲ St Mark's Basilica shows Byzantine elements such as golden mosaics and thoughtfully placed windows. Sunlight would bathe the mosaics and give the church a holy atmosphere

ANCIENT & MEDIEVAL ARCHITECTURE

 ## St Basil the Blessed

One of the most recognisable landmarks of Russia is the multicoloured, nine-towered Cathedral of St Basil the Blessed. It was built to celebrate Tsar Ivan IV's victory over the Tatars (Mongols). This cathedral is the only Byzantine construction of its millennium. It was built over c.1554–60, by when the Byzantine era was long over in western Europe.

 ## An Asymmetrical Gem

The Cathedral of St Basil is built in eccentric shapes. It is formed by eight chapels surrounding a central ninth chapel. This central chapel—the Church of the Intercession of the Mother of God—has a tall, tent-like tower for a roof. The four largest domes sit on top of octagonal towers. These domes cover the Church of St Cyprian and St Justina, Church of the Holy Trinity, Church of the Icon of St Nicholas the Miracle Worker, and the Church of the Entry of the Lord into Jerusalem. The **motley** roofs rise to a spire from an onion-shaped dome.

▲ *The Cathedral of Vasily the Blessed, or Saint Basil's, in the Red Square in Moscow, Russia*

▲ *The lavish interior at St Basil*

 ## The Holy Fool

The cathedral's name comes from the Russian holy fool Vasily Blazhenny (St Basil the Blessed) who was a 'fool for Christ'. He is buried in the church vaults.

👤 In Real Life

The site of the Hagia Sophia was first occupied by a pagan temple. It later became the site of Constantine I's cathedral Megale Ekklesia. And still later, Justinian's Hagia Sophia. In 1453, Ottoman Sultan Mehmed II converted the Hagia Sophia into a mosque. In 1943, the Turkish Republic's first president made the Hagia Sophia a secular building. It is now no longer a temple, church or mosque, but a museum.

Chinese Architecture

China is geographically vast, culturally diverse and historically rich. In comparison, its architecture shows little variation. This is because, from very early on, imperial governments set codes and standards for buildings throughout the nation. They were also influenced by **Confucian** and Buddhist philosophies.

◀ Dragons are found everywhere across China—in wood, jade, stone and ceramic. They were seen as a symbol of royalty. Anyone else who dared use dragons could be put to death as a criminal

▲ The Yungang Grottoes are 53 caves with exquisite carvings of gods and demons. They were built into sandstone cliffs by Buddhist monks over 50 years during the 5th century

Structure and Order

Chinese people often lived in large families. So, Chinese homes had a number of buildings. These buildings were located in a single enclosure with one or more courtyards. Important buildings, such as ancestral and religious halls, would face the front of the property. Servants' rooms, storage houses and kitchens were kept at the farthest sides.

▶ The Great Wall of China in the mountains near Beijing

The Great Wall

You could say all of China is an enclosure. The First Emperor of China built the first Great Wall. Later emperors maintained and added to the wall. What you see now is in fact a series of walls running from northern China to southern Mongolia. Often there are multiple walls running parallel to each other.

The wall was built from whatever building materials were locally available. This included wooden boards, bricks, rubble, rocks and stones. The outside parapet is generally **crenellated**. The inside part of the wall is lowered, to stop people and horses from accidentally falling off the edge.

Thousands of slaves, prisoners, soldiers and local people gave their lives to build and re-build the wall. Many of them lie buried in the wall, which has long been seen as a symbol of oppression and tyranny. What is worse, the wall did not stop the invaders.

ANCIENT & MEDIEVAL ARCHITECTURE

The Forbidden City

China's main palace lies in a massive walled-off area in Beijing. It is called Zijin Cheng (the Forbidden City). It is divided into the Outer and Inner Courts. The Outer Court occupies the southern area. It was used for public and ceremonial functions. Its most important buildings also face south, to honour the Sun. The Inner Court contains the palaces of the emperor and his family. You can tell how important a building is by its height, width, style of the roof and the number of figurines on the roof.

▲ Beyond the main gate lies the Golden River, which runs across a vast courtyard. The Gate of Supreme Harmony lies at the end of the courtyard. It leads to the Outer Court

▲ Palace of Tranquil Longevity in the Forbidden City, the palace of the Chinese emperor

▲ Having 10 mythical beasts on the roof indicates that this building (the Hall of Supreme Harmony) has the highest status in the whole empire

Potala Palace

Tibetan architects took Indian and Chinese elements and changed them into an entirely unique style. The Potala Palace—the official home of the Dalai Lama—is an example of this rare architecture. Covering a massive 36 hectares, it contains 1,000 rooms and 10,000 shrines. The building rises 117 metres above a hill. It is a stepped construction of stone and timber.

◀ The Potala Palace

Islamic Architecture

From the 7th to the 17th century, Islamic architecture spread across Asia, Africa and Europe. Muslim architects were forbidden by holy law to show the image of God or living beings in their creations. Thus, they created buildings without statues and murals. Instead, they focussed on symmetry, tile-work and **calligraphy**. Their utterly amazing buildings include the Dome of the Rock, Samarra's Great Mosque, Cordoba's Great Mosque, Topkapi Palace and Fatehpur Sikhri, to name a few.

Jerusalem's Dome of the Rock

▲ *Qubbet Es-Sakra (Dome of the Rock)*

Built over the rock from which Prophet Mohammad rose to heaven, Dome of the Rock is one of Islam's earliest monuments. The octagonal structure shows Syrian Byzantine influence. It has Roman columns and intricate **mosaics**.

▶ *Samarra's Great Mosque was once the largest mosque in the world. It has a spiralling minaret and is supported by semi-circular towers. Its enormous **arcaded** courtyard can hold 80,000 people*

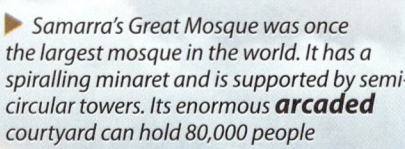

An Umayyad Dynasty Mosque

The glorious Great Mosque at Cordoba is best known for its amazing prayer hall. It has 850 granite, jasper and marble columns. These support striped horseshoe-shaped arches. Sunlight and lamp-light filter through, casting hypnotic patterns across the floor.

▲ *Cordoba's Great Mosque: 200 years in construction*

ANCIENT & MEDIEVAL ARCHITECTURE   19

Standalone Minarets

In Islam, a muezzin calls the faithful to prayer from the balcony of a minaret, five times a day. Among the tallest minarets in Asia is the 72.5-m-high Qutb Minar. It is a tapering, richly carved sandstone tower. Each floor shows projecting balconies. Exquisite marble work covers the base.

Minarets have a base, cap, shaft and a head. They are seen in many grand mosques, like the Great Mosque of Testour. Minarets are also seen in the Taj Mahal.

▲ Qutb Minar, Delhi

▲ Filigreed screens added elegance to windows, arches, verandas and other palatial structures. The filigreed balcony above this wooden column bore the throne of Emperor Akbar at Fatehpur Sikhri, India

Taj Mahal

A perfectly symmetrical layout of domes, arches and minarets in white marble makes the Taj Mahal a marvel of Islamic-Indian architecture. Inside, the **mausoleum** is octagonal. It has ornate carvings and floral designs. These are set in semiprecious stones, such as lapis lazuli, jade, crystal, amethyst and turquoise. Two buildings of red sandstone stand on either side of the mausoleum. At the southern end is a red and white gateway with arches and cupola. These structures offer a striking contrast to the white marble tomb.

▲ The Taj Mahal is set in classical Mughal gardens. These feature waterways, fountains, ornamental trees and walking paths

Alhambra

The fortress palace of Alhambra is one of the finest achievements of the Spanish Moors. It is set on a lush plateau overlooking a steep ravine. The land is planted with oranges, roses, myrtle and other fragrant and ornamental plants. Within the fortress are grand courts, palaces, a throne room, fountains, columns and halls.

▼ Moorish poets described the fortress of Alhambra as a 'pearl set in emeralds', referring to the amazing colours of its palaces and woods

▲ The home of 30 Ottoman sultans, Topkapi Palace shows the multiple influences of an expanding empire. It is built in Islamic, Ottoman and European styles. Its pointed arches became a standard feature of Gothic architecture in Europe

Architecture of the Indian Subcontinent

Ancient and medieval India created some of the most enthralling architecture in the world. This was influenced by Hindu, Buddhist, Jain, Sikh, Islamic and many other philosophies. The buildings celebrate nature and the supernatural. They show worldly pleasures and otherworldly pastimes. Above all, they reflect a love for divinity. To share such an abundance of stories, Indian architects built vast, maze-like, intricately decorated monuments. It can often be hard to figure out where to start exploring or what to look at first!

▶ *The Meenakshi Temple at Madurai in southern India has 14 multi-storied gopuram (towering gateways) packed with incredible statuary. The four largest gopuram serve as the main gateways into this labyrinthine temple*

▶ *Harmandir Sahib, more popularly called the Golden Temple, is the chief gurudwara of Sikhs. Built in marble and copper, it is most notable for its gleaming gold-foil facade*

Tiered Towers

Many Indian temples are built with towers called *shikhara* or *vimana*. They are usually seen rising above the sanctuary or pillared halls. A gopuram is a soaring pyramid-like gateway to the temple. Almost all towers have multiple layers. On the outside, they are carved with scenes from legends and local history. The inner walls are sometimes decorated with murals.

▼ *This rooftop belongs to the monolithic temple of Kailasha. It is a part of 34 monasteries and temples cut into a cliff face at Ellora. These shrines show Buddhist, Hindu and Jain styles*

ANCIENT & MEDIEVAL ARCHITECTURE

Stupa

Often seen in Buddhist and Jain architecture, stupas are large domes that sometimes house sacred relics. The most famous one is the Great Stupa at Sanchi, which was built by Mauryan emperor Ashoka to honour the Buddha. The monument has four gateways, richly carved with scenes from the *Jataka* tales and the life of the Buddha.

Hoysala Architecture

The Hoysala Empire's unique architectural style is marked by attention to symmetry and detail. Located by the Kaveri River, the Chennakeshava Temple at Somanathapura is an excellent example. Its *trikuta* (three-shrine) complex is built in a 16-point star shape and is teeming with figurines.

▲ *The Great Stupa at Sanchi is one of the oldest stone structures in India*

◀ *Shrines at Chennakeshava sit on raised platforms, a common Hoysala feature. Each shrine has its own vimana*

◀ *There are several reliefs and wall carvings on the walls of the Hoysala Temple. They depict various scenes from Hindu lore, including battles between the Hindu gods, important events, etc.*

Isn't It Amazing!

Emperor Ashoka came to the throne when Buddhism was still new to the world. After one of his victorious but bloodiest wars, the Emperor was overcome with remorse for the carnage he had caused. He determined never again to raise arms and instead to conquer using compassion, mercy and non-violence. He upheld Buddhist values and helped spread it across the land.

▶ *The symbol of the four lions is used on Indian currency*

Pillared Places

Pillared corridors and chambers are a hallmark of Hindu architecture. A *mandapa* is a pillared hall. The most awe-inspiring *mandapa* are built just outside the sanctuary or in between shrines. An *ardha-mandapa* is a porch-like entrance to some temples. *Bhoga mandapa* is used to prepare food for the gods in certain temples. *Nata mandapa* is a dance hall, seen in palaces and temples.

▶ *The shrines of many large temples are surrounded by never-ending, stone-pillared corridors, as seen in the Sthanumalayar Temple of Suchindaram, in southern India. The corridors were lit up (in the evenings) by lamp-bearing maidens carved onto the columns*

Heritage of Southeast Asia

The architecture of Southeast Asia shows strong Buddhist and Hindu influence. Indian elements such as the *stupa*, the *shikhara*, and the flower and animal motifs rapidly spread across Myanmar, Thailand, Cambodia and Indonesia. Architects of these regions added their own creative touches and gave birth to breathtaking new designs.

▲ Rich and massive spires were much loved in Southeast Asia. These are seen at Myanmar's Shwedagon Pagoda, where many gold pagodas surround a 113-m-high spire

▲ Southeast Asia is a melting pot of cultures. In central Thailand, you can see the Theravada Buddhist temple Wat Amon Yat (left) alongside a Chinese folk-religion temple (right)

Borobudur

The gigantic and extraordinary Buddhist monument of Borobudur was built in Java over 778–850 CE. It is created to resemble Mount Meru, a holy Hindu mountain. Borobudur's form is symbolic of the *mandala*—a symbol of the universe that uses squares for the earth and circles for heaven. The entire structure is festooned with stupas and statues of the Buddha.

▶ The stone blocks of Borobudur express religious and secular scenes. This relief shows the king and queen granting an audience to their subjects

Enlightenment at Borobudur

Built from volcanic stone, the pyramid-like Borobudur encloses a hillock. It consists of three main levels, divided into nine lesser levels. There is a square base, five square terraces in the middle, and three circular terraces on the upper level. The central stupa is 35 metre in height. Each level represents a stage on the path to enlightenment. A pilgrim enters from the eastern staircase, then mimics the spiritual journey by walking clockwise up the levels to reach the top. The total distance is more than 5 kilometres!

▲ The Karmavibanga carving at Borobudur expresses the Buddhist belief that those who harm living beings—even such mute creatures as turtles and fish—will be punished in hell

▲ The steep stairway at Borobudur leads pilgrims to Kamadhatu (realm of desire). From here, pilgrims move to Rupadhatu (realm of forms and shapes) and to the highest planes of Arupadhatu (realm of formlessness)

ANCIENT & MEDIEVAL ARCHITECTURE

🏛 Angkor Wat

Built in the 12th century by King Suryavarman II, Angkor Wat marks the pinnacle of the Khmer Empire's architecture. It is the largest religious complex in the word. Spread across 160 hectares, it is laid out according to the Hindu temple-mountain plan. The temple has five central towers that represent the peaks of Mount Meru. The mountain is surrounded by a vast and complex moat that symbolises the mythical 'ocean at the edge of the world'. One enters Angkor Wat by crossing a 188-m-long bridge. On the way to the temple are three galleries, separated from each other by paved walkways.

◀ Angkor Wat surrounded by the moat representing the world ocean. Angkor Wat was intended by King Suryavarman II to be the resting place for his mortal remains. The holy images covering its walls include the much-admired Churning of the Ocean, which depicts Vishnu in his Kuruma avatar, surrounded by gods and demigods

🏛 Religious Motifs

Angkor Wat is dedicated to the gods Brahma, Vishnu and Shiva. It is filled with Hindu motifs. The walls have sculptures of exquisite quality. These depict scenes from ancient Khmer (modern Cambodia) as well as scenes from the heroic Hindu epics *Mahabharata* and *Ramayana*.

▼ Carvings at the nearby temple of Bayon in Angkor Thom shows charging elephants in a battle. This battle, between Cham and Khmer, was conducted by King Jayavarman VII

▼ Gigantic, serene stone heads are a hallmark of Khmer architecture

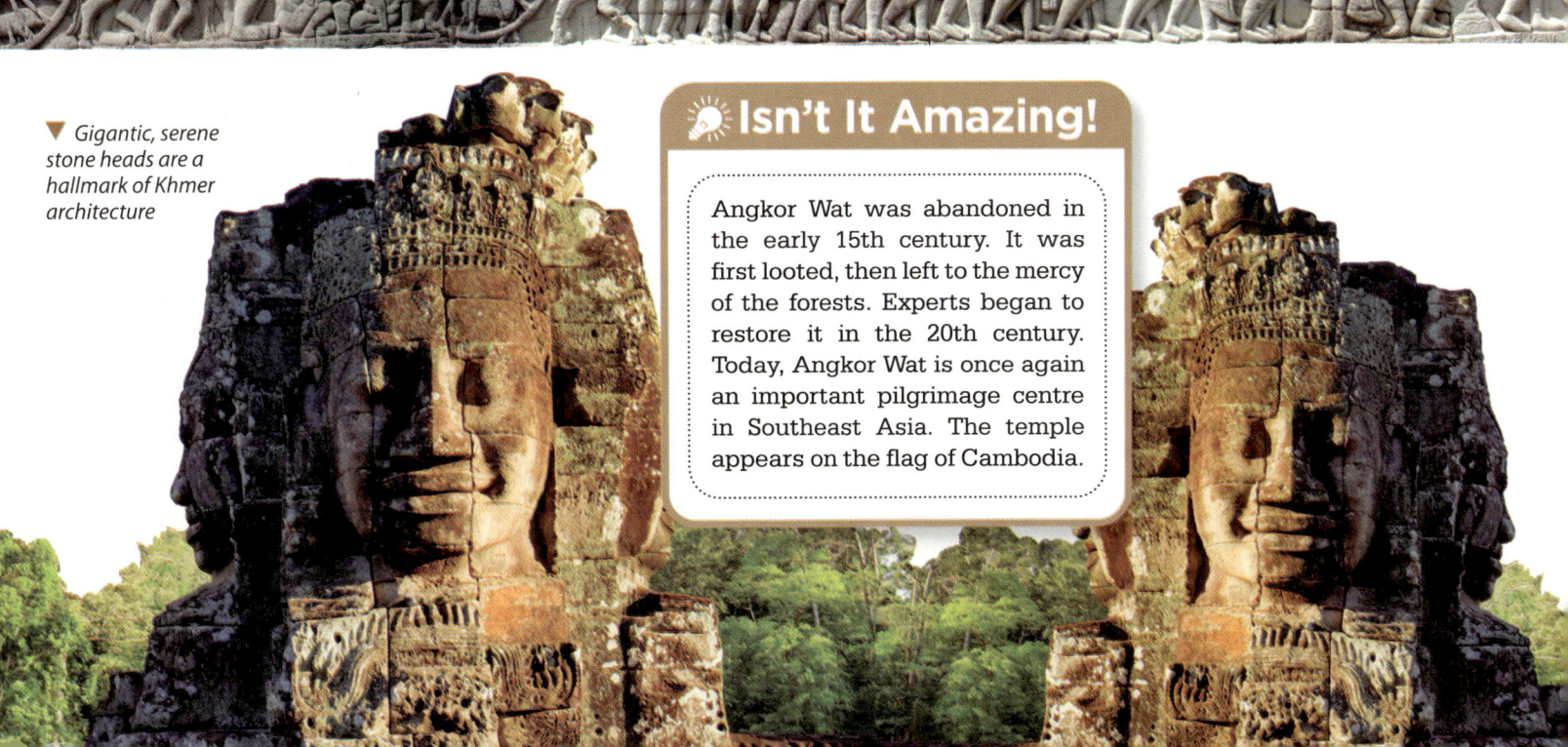

💡 Isn't It Amazing!

Angkor Wat was abandoned in the early 15th century. It was first looted, then left to the mercy of the forests. Experts began to restore it in the 20th century. Today, Angkor Wat is once again an important pilgrimage centre in Southeast Asia. The temple appears on the flag of Cambodia.

Dynamic Japan

The islands of Japan are prone to earthquakes and volcanic eruptions. Traditional homes in Japan were made to be easily reassembled if they collapsed. Gardens too, play a great part in Japanese architecture. They accompany large homes, temples and tea houses. The largest buildings were often castles made from timber and sturdy blocks of stone.

▲ Old Japanese buildings of wood were raised off the ground. This Phoenix Hall (Hoo-do) was built in 1053 CE and shows tiled roofs and a Chinese influence

Tea Ceremonies

The Way of Tea is honoured in Japan with special tea houses (*cha-shitsu*) set in serene gardens. Cha-shitsu are usually wooden pavilions with thatched roofs. The walls have large openings that are protected by sliding doors covered with paper. The translucent paper lets in gentle light, setting the atmosphere for drinking tea.

▶ *Choshukaku tea pavilion at the Sankeien garden. Tea pavilions have no furniture. In fact, no traditional Japanese house does. People usually sit on the floor on cushions or mats*

Shinto Shrines

The Way of the Kami (divine beings) is better known as the religion Shinto. The *torii* is the iconic gateway to Shinto temples. The *kami* lives in the inner shrine, the *honden*. People worship in a hall called the *haiden*. Large shrines have other rooms, such as a hall for ritual dancing (*kaguraden*).

Castles

Japan's warrior classes built massive fortresses, of which the best preserved is the Himeji Castle. Built strategically on a hill, the castle is guarded by 15-metre-high sloping stone walls. Its 84 small gates limited enemy entrance. Additional protection came from three water-filled moats. Inside, winding passages confused enemy infiltrators. High up in the walls, openings (*ishiotoshi*) and holes (*sama*) allowed defenders to hurl stones or scalding water and fire arrows.

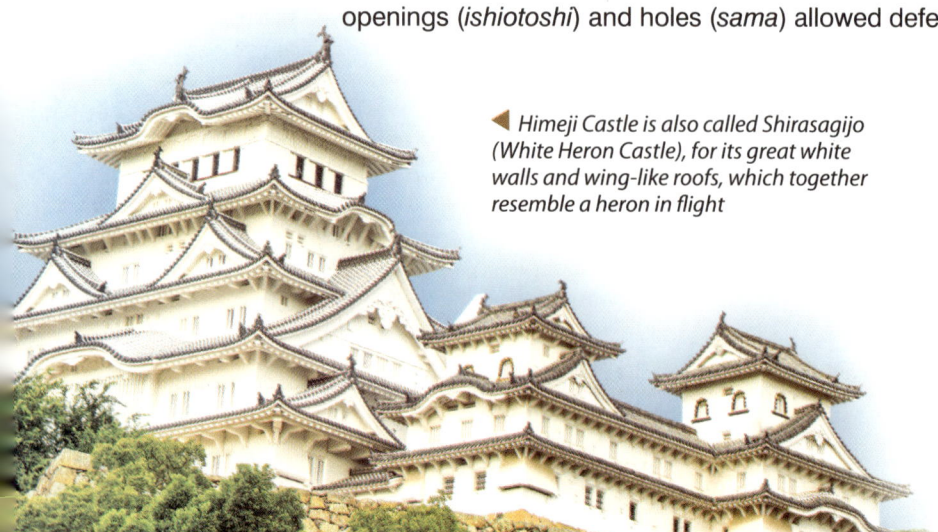

◀ *Himeji Castle is also called Shirasagijo (White Heron Castle), for its great white walls and wing-like roofs, which together resemble a heron in flight*

Kinkaku-ji Temple

The Golden Pavillion (Kinkaku-ji) of Kyoto expresses three styles of Japanese architecture. The ground floor is in a 14th-century domestic style called *Shinden-zukuri*. The first floor reflects samurai-style houses. The top floor, called *Kukyocho* (Cupola of the Ultimate), is built in Zen style.

ANCIENT & MEDIEVAL ARCHITECTURE

Japanese Gardens

Traditional gardens in Japan mimic nature. They follow simple, harmonious designs. Most gardens were created for relaxation and meditation. Priests in particular studied how to make beautiful gardens. They gave Buddhist names to different parts of their landscape. They even followed Buddhist ideas while designing gardens.

► Spring blossoms on a Japanese cherry tree (sakura)

Kansho

Gardens built for contemplation are called *kansho*. The entire scenery can be enjoyed by sitting in one place, which is specially constructed for this purpose.

Funasobi and Shuyu

Gardens meant to be explored by boat are called *funasobi*. These were usually built around a large pond. The estate around Byodo-in is laid out in this style. Gardens built especially for strolling through are called *shuyu*. The most pleasing sceneries here are discovered as you walk along the constructed path. Bridges cross lakes to ensure a continuous walkway.

▲ Autumn colours at the gardens of Daigo-ji temple, Tokyo

▲ Stone pathway across a pond filled with lotus leaves

▲ The amazing gardens at the Katsura Imperial Villa combine areas for strolling, boating and meditation

Rock Gardens

Both Shinto and Buddhist shrines use sand and gravel to create unique rock gardens. In Zen Buddhism, rock-garden patterns express water and clouds. White sand is used to show purity. Stones are placed to mark islands or mountains in the garden. Altogether, these elements symbolise the beauty and mystery of nature.

Bonsai

An ancient Japanese art, bonsai literally means 'planting in a tray'. It is the method by which dwarf trees are grown. The trees are in fact normal trees, but they are grown in a way that the roots, trunk, branches and leaves age without growing large. The best bonsai look like mature trees but are small enough to fit in a tray.

◄ Once the practice of specialists alone, the bonsai tree is commonly grown today

Pre-Columbian Americas

Before the 16th century, the Americas had thriving and sophisticated civilisations. Their cities and culture were largely destroyed, and later rediscovered by European settlers. The best-known architectural remains belong to the Mayans, Incans and Aztecs.

Pre-Aztec Teotihuacan

One of the largest and best-preserved Mesoamerican cities is Teotihuacan (The City of the Gods). It holds plazas, temples, palaces, some 2,000 apartments and even a canal. The broadest road is the 40-m-wide Avenue of the Dead. At the northern end of the road are amazing stepped pyramids. The largest is the 43-m-high Pyramid of the Moon. Along the Avenue's southern part is the citadel a square courtyard that is home to the Temple of Quetzalcoatl, the Feathered Serpent.

▲ Avenue of the Dead, with the Pyramid of the Moon and lesser stepped pyramids

Codz-Poop: The Palace of Masks

Mayan architecture has a fascinating variety of elements. The remains of the Palace of Masks show a close matrix of grotesques and masks, in a style called Puuc. The name 'Codz-Poop' means 'rolled blanket'. Though the interiors of the Codz-Poop have not survived the passage of time, the exterior is still impressive. Lots of ruins from the Mayan buildings have simple facades, but Codz-Poop is different. The outside is covered with stones that are shaped like the face of the god of rain.

◀ The Temple of Warriors at Chichen Itza, Mexico, is one of the few remaining examples of colonnaded (hypostyle) halls in Mayan architecture

Ancestral Pueblo

Some of the most amazing architecture can be seen in the cliff dwellings of the Ancestral Puebloans of south-western USA. These were most likely built between 1150 CE and 1300 CE. The rooms often had 'doors' on the roof. People climbed up to the roof using ladders, and then came down to the floor through a hole in the ceiling! Each community had two or more *kivas* (ceremonial rooms) that were round, but became square in later times.

◀ The Ancient Pueblo homes of the Cliff Palace at Mesa Verde National Park in Colorado

ANCIENT & MEDIEVAL ARCHITECTURE

Machu Picchu

Hidden in the Andes mountain range, the ruins of Machu Picchu were once the palace city of the Inca ruler Pachacuti Inca Yupanqui (ruled c. 1438–71 CE). Walking paths and stone steps were carved into mountains which connected ancient plazas, homes, terraces, graveyards and major buildings. These include the Temple of the Sun and its Military Tower, the temples of the Apollo district, the Princess Palace and the Palace of the Inca. On three sides, Machu Picchu is bordered by stepped farming terraces, once watered by aqueducts.

Chan Chan, Peru

The largest city in pre-Columbian America was the capital of the Chimu Kingdom (c. 1100–1470 CE), Chan Chan. It was built using adobe brick and finished with mud. The exteriors were often decorated with patterned reliefs and **arabesques**. The city centre held many walled citadels where aristocrats most likely lived. Their cemeteries and storehouses were also in the same area. Each citadel contained pyramidal temples, gardens, water tanks and symmetrical rooms.

▼ Machu Picchu is a Peruvian Historical Sanctuary and a UNESCO World Heritage Site. One of the New Seven Wonders of the World

▲ Reliefs at Primera Plaza (First Square), Chan Chan

▲ Once the largest city in the Americas, the site of the Chan Chan is in ruins today

Romanesque Architecture

Around the time of King Charlemagne (r. 768–814 CE), Christian basilicas in French areas began to grow larger. These were needed to take in the growing numbers of Christian monks and pilgrims. Larger buildings had to be more thoughtfully constructed, so they would not be crushed by their own weight. Successful new designs began to spread across Europe. Soon, they were applied to other types of buildings. Between the 10th and 11th centuries, these styles developed into what is called Romanesque architecture. It includes formidable masonry (stonework), vaulted ceilings, semicircular arches, unique sculptures and bell towers.

Aachen Cathedral

The Palatine (royal) Chapel at Aachen Cathedral shows early development of Romanesque architecture. This includes lofty galleries, semicircular arches and Classical columns.

◀ *Charlemagne's Palatine Chapel at Aachen Cathedral, Germany*

▲ *Built by European crusaders, Krak des Chevaliers is a medieval fortress. Its massive walls and few, small windows are typical of Romanesque castles*

▶ *The Romanesque desire for arcades reached its peak at the Pisa Cathedral. Its famous leaning tower is built with continuous arcading all the way to the top*

▼ *The Abbey of Saint-Etienne is a Romanesque monastery founded by William the Conqueror*

ANCIENT & MEDIEVAL ARCHITECTURE

Ornamental sculpture

Inside, Romanesque churches show masonry with floral and geometrical decorations. Notably, the tympanum—the half-moon space just below an arch—was used to depict figures from the Bible.

▲ *Corbels representing the sins of lust, gluttony and sloth*

▶ *Groin-vaulted colonnade of the cloister at the Old Cathedral of Coimbra, Portugal*

Columns

Romanesque buildings were not only gigantic, they were made of stone (rather than wood). Columns had to bear greater weights. Thus, sturdy drum-like cylinders became popular. Some were even hollow and filled with leftover stone rubble. Alternating columns and piers (load-bearing walls) also helped to distribute the weight.

Vaults

Romanesque buildings were often topped with lofty vaults of stone or brick. The simplest version is the barrel vault—a single arched ceiling that extends from wall to wall. A groin vault is generally square-shaped and built by the intersection of two barrel vaults at right angles. They are often seen in crypts and church aisles.

▶ *A barrel-vaulted ceiling with its original medieval paintings*

Gothic Architecture

Over the 12th and 14th centuries, Christian and secular styles of Europe came together in the spectacular Gothic style of architecture. This is marked by soaring buildings that reflect a yearning for the heavens. Every part of it, both inside and outside, is crammed with fantastic sculptures, intricate pointed arches, miraculous rib-vaulted ceilings, tall windows and exquisite stained glass. The truly enormous cathedrals were made possible by an engineering breakthrough called flying buttresses. Altogether, Gothic architecture is an amazing mesh of religion, philosophy and art.

▲ Gothic sculptures showed a never-before-seen range of iconography. Architects used them liberally both inside and on the facades of buildings

Flying Buttresses

A buttress is a structure that adds stability to a building. Flying buttresses are made from bars of stone that arch outwards ('fly' out) from the upper walls to a supporting wall (pier). Such buttresses carry the outward pressure placed on walls by heavy roofs. This design allowed the creation of skyrocketing cathedrals, typical of Gothic architecture.

▲ These grim figures with water spouts (often opening out at the mouths) are called gargoyles. They were useful for draining out rain water or channelling fountains

▲ The buttresses at the Notre Dame Cathedral in Paris hold the building up with a deceptively delicate pincer-like hold that is pleasing to the eye

ANCIENT & MEDIEVAL ARCHITECTURE

 ## Gothic Arches

Simple pointed windows, called lancets, are a Gothic hallmark. Later Gothic windows show increasing subdivisions of the window (known as mullions) and elaborate tracery.

▶ *Lancet windows at Ripon Cathedral, Yorkshire*

 ## Rayonnant Style

The height of Gothic architecture, Rayonnant is less about size and more about decoration. Architects in the 13th century became bolder with pinnacles, mouldings and window tracery. Buttresses became more elegant and windows became larger. The topmost walls (between the ceiling and the arches) were entirely replaced with one long, continuous screen of mullioned windows, tracery and stained glass. These filtered a gentle light into the vast inner spaces, creating an ethereal atmosphere.

In Real Life

The ethereal beauty inside a Gothic cathedral comes from the soft rainbow light due to its large stained-glass windows. Strange to say, the imperfect glass of the Middle Ages—that is, glass with little bubbles of air trapped in them—is far more brilliant than the smooth, clear glass of modern times. This is because the air bubbles catch and reflect more light and dazzle the eye

▲ *York Minster Rose Window*

 ## Gothic Ceilings

The stability offered by pointed arches and flying buttresses allowed architects to be more creative with vaulted ceilings. New, intricate systems of stone ribs were developed that looked spectacular. They also distributed the weight more evenly between columns and piers, all the way to the ground. Masons were able to make vaults with lighter, thinner stone, so the walls could be opened up to ever-larger windows.

◀ *The high Gothic facade of St Vitus Cathedral, with tall mullioned windows and intricate detailing*

Word Check

Abaton: It refers to an ancient Greek enclosure in the temple of Asclepios where patients slept.

Adobe: It is clay-like material used for building structures.

Amphitheatre: It is a circular building with rising levels of seating (as seen in a football stadium)

Arabesques: It is an intricate floral pattern, sometimes with animals and figures included.

Arcade: It is an arched, covered passageway or gallery.

Barracks: It is a place where soldiers are housed.

Calligraphy: The art of beautiful handwriting.

Caravanserai: It is an Eastern hotel with overnight parking space for caravans.

Confucian: A person who believes in the teachings of the Chinese philosopher Confucius.

Corbels: It is a structure that sticks out from a wall and supports weight.

Crenellated: It is a defensive wall into which gaps (crenels) are added. The gaps were used to bombard enemy soldiers with missiles.

Filigreed: Delicate ornamental work made of fine wire

Gypsum: It is a material used in the making of plaster of Paris and drywall.

Hieroglyph: An image of an object representing a word

Iconography: It describes the images and symbols that are associated with religious and legendary figures.

Mausoleum: It is a building that houses one or more tombs.

Mosaics: They are decorations made by putting together different coloured tiles to form a pattern.

Motley: Multi-coloured; often a bright contrasting mix of colours

Nabatean: It is an ancient Arab kingdom.

Pastoral: It is related to the open green countryside; rural, not urban.

Pedestal: It is the base or foot of a column.

Pharaohs: Ancient Egypt's rulers who were the political and religious heads of the state

Porphyry: It is a large rock containing crystals of quartz or feldspar.

Roundels: It is a round object, like a window or a decorative plate.

Ventilation: It is a system for providing fresh air.